12-2-74

V. Gilbert Beers has the gift of seeing commonplace objects and everyday events with a deeply sensitive eye, alive to the eternal beauty of God's universe, aware of the complete happiness that comes to all who accept His love. The author's special magic infuses familiar scenes of family life with fresh insights and clarity, unjaded by the passage of time, tinged by the spark of true reverence.

Reading the daily newspaper, breakfasting with his family, holding hands with his wife under the table, regret for lost hours, watching an errant squirrel in the backyard, rereading old books, studying raindrops on the windowpane with his children, administering a spanking (well-deserved but, oh, so painful to Daddy), enjoying the beauty of a single tree, recalling Christmases past, rueful over a bulging appointment book, family solidarity, joy at the coming of Spring, reminiscences of his childhood on a farm, the sudden beauty of sunrise, anxious moments while hurrying to catch a plane, a twinge of sadness at spying a worn-out teddy bear on the trash heap, parting with tears from loved ones, reuniting with untold happiness. And finally, the ultimate experience: the joy of Jesus, on the Cross where He completed the work of redemption, and the joy which His presence brings to all who know Him.

Along with sketches of daily life, abounding with joy for those who are willing to seek and find, Dr. Beers has included poetic passages and excerpts from Scripture that are particularly meaningful to

By V. Gilbert Beers

PATTERNS FOR PRAYER FROM THE GOSPELS
JOY IS. . . .

each situation. Together with the author's creative style and unpretentious attitudes, these elements combine to make a book of unusual relevance, deep inspiration, and refreshing joy.

> "I prayed for joy,
>   but He sent love instead,
>   His love, and that of others,
>   that I might take it,
>   and with it get
>   the gift of joy, too."

*How to discover the prayerful presence of joy
in our daily lives*
V. Gilbert Beers

Fleming H. Revell Company
Old Tappan, New Jersey

All Scripture quotations in this volume are from the King James Version of the Bible.

Library of Congress Cataloging in Publication Data

Beers, Victor Gilbert,
Joy is. . . .

1. Joy—Meditations. I. Title.
BV4905.2.B35   242   74–9780
ISBN 0–8007–0677–3

1835737

Contents

Introduction

Joy is not searching for suffering.
Joy is not enduring suffering.
Joy is not suffering itself.
Joy is working for Jesus and His friends,
    even when it requires suffering.
Joy is persevering for Jesus and His friends,
    despite suffering.
Joy is the patient persistence in the Lord's work,
    no matter what the cost.
Joy is Jesus working in your life,
    taking you through suffering, trials,
    and temptation to victory.

Newspapers

I don't know why I bother to read the newspaper every day. But I do.

This morning it took me by the nape of the neck and dragged me through the back alleys of life. It always does. There isn't much time spent trying to make life look pretty.

But I'm tired of dreary news.

Who cares if the price of gold in Bongo-Bongo is five dollars less per ounce than it was the day before? I've enough worries with yesterday's car-repair bill and the mortgage payment coming up next week.

So the stock market fell another thirteen points. And Joe Schmaltz beat his wife and she sued him for divorce. Then there's always some article about a greedy fellow who got caught with his hand in the cash register.

No, I'm tired of this kind of news. It keeps pouring in every day. And, like an idiot, I keep reading it.

What am I? A creature of habit? A little machine that I've built myself, programmed to do the same thing each day, no matter how edifying it is? Why do I force myself to read the same thing every day? Only the names and places change, but the plot is stereotyped.

Tomorrow Joe Schmaltz will be anonymous. The world will not care a nickel about his wife or her beating, or Joe either. The papers won't print the story of Joe's reconciliation. No, that's not news.

Yet, tomorrow I'll be there with a fresh paper, gulping down another story about another Joe Schmaltz, in another place, playing out a slightly different role.

But this morning I caught myself in the act. That wasn't all. I caught myself with a smug smile on my face.

"I don't beat my wife," I was saying. "She hasn't sued me for divorce. As a matter of fact, we haven't even argued lately."

It wasn't that I enjoyed the bad news. No, I just felt good that I wasn't like Joe Schmaltz. I knew that if all the Joes behaved like me there wouldn't be a morning newspaper. There wouldn't be enough bad news to print.

Then I got caught up into Joe's shoes, trying to think how he must feel. Poor Joe! I felt terrible, thinking about hurting my wife. Worse than that, being separated from her.

Suddenly I was hungry for forgiveness and reconciliation. Here I was, Joe Schmaltz, running to my wife and begging her for forgiveness. My heart felt warm and tender as she threw her arms around me and we mingled our tears.

Then something happened.

I suddenly felt a sense of joy which the real me hadn't felt for a while. Strange. Joe Schmaltz, the wife beater, bathing in a newfound joy which I had missed in my "proper" life.

It almost made me want to beat up my wife to discover this joy for myself!

Then it hit me. I don't have to beat up my wife. I threw down the newspaper and ran out to the kitchen.

You can imagine her surprise when I threw my arms around her and kissed her on the ear. "Honey," I said softly. "Have I hurt you in any way lately?"

"As a matter of fact," she said, "you're absolutely killing my left foot. Would you please put your big size elevens somewhere else? And while you're at it, will you please pull your tie out of the pancake batter. It would taste awful."

"No, no! I mean it," I said. Then I told her about Joe Schmaltz and the way I'd taken his place in my mind. "If I've hurt you in any way, I'm sorry. Forgive me!"

"Dum Dum!" she crooned. "Did you bring my pancakes to a halt just to tell me that?" Then she threw her arms around me and I felt one hot tear drop on my arm.

We held each other for a while and I felt that warm sense of joy that I had felt as Joe Schmaltz. It was just as real as if we had straightened out some pretty horrible things between us.

Really, those pancakes did taste better that morning. But have you ever tried eating them while you're holding hands under the table?

My Needs and Yours

I have needs.
You have needs.
God has all the riches
To supply those needs.
I recognize your needs.
I grow concerned for your needs
Because I love you.
I pray for those needs.
I ask God to give you His riches
So that you will be less poor.
God gives you riches
And you *are* less poor.
But I receive the joy.
The God of joy has heard me.
He has answered me.
He has supplied your needs.
But now I am richer
Than I was before,
Not because I asked for riches,
But because I asked for you to be richer.
Through my prayer
I cashed a check
In the Bank of Heaven,
And put it into your account.
But in doing this,
I found that God had cashed a bigger one
And put it into my account.
Through my prayer,
I involved myself in your affairs
And God's.

And touched the heartstrings of both
And made them my affair.
Through my prayer,
I did something about you
And your need,
And God did something, too.
You need my prayers and God's supplies.
God wants your needs and my prayers.
And I need the gift of joy
That comes through praying for you.

The joy that you bring as I pray for you is told in
1 Thessalonians 3:9.

Strength and Weakness

I prayed for joy,
   but He sent weakness
   and brought me low
   until I reached up to Him to help
   and then I found
   His strength, and joy.

Lost Hours

Lord, let's talk about those lost hours.

There are so many of them. I simply can't account for them all. I know You could remind me of each one, and I'm ashamed that they're so important to You and so unimportant to me.

How could I let so many slip by? No, no! Please don't answer that. I think I know. But I would rather not have You remind me.

Let's see. I lost forty minutes commuting this morning. A little music, a little news, not all lost time, but I don't feel especially uplifted because of it.

And what about the twenty minutes I lost waiting for my first client? Not much to do in the waiting room, except thumb through some outdated magazines and make some small talk with the receptionist about the noisy street repairs in front of the building.

Those three taxi trips were certainly lost hours, Lord. I couldn't read. The drivers grumbled about muggings, and people who didn't pay their fares, and some who didn't tip.

Lord, I can't get that one taxi trip off my mind. The one where I was late to an appointment and had to eat a hamburger in the backseat of the cab. Of course, it was stupid of me, but in my hurry, I left my gloves behind, the ones my wife had given me for Christmas. You know how much time I spent trying to get them back. But I never did.

We could talk, too, about the time spent on that proposal for a company that never intended to do anything about it anyway. Of course I didn't know that then, Lord. And I didn't know that the other company was delaying because of internal power struggles.

But those seemed like such wasted hours.

Lord, the thing that frightens me is the way these lost hours add up. A few here, a few there. But a month of them! It's staggering. How can I keep them from being lost hours?

I want to redeem some of them. Cash them in. Not for money, necessarily. Just for something worthwhile. What can I do, Lord, to get some genuine joy from them?

Could I spend time in a taxi talking with You? Or while I'm waiting for my next client to call me in? Or while I'm commuting to work? That's a thought!

It's been some time since I memorized a verse from Your Word, Lord. Now why didn't I think about that before? Why couldn't I spend some of these lost hours learning one verse each day from Your Word? Think of it! That's 365 verses in a year.

You know that I'm always complaining that I don't have time to think about You, Lord. I just never have time to meditate and reflect on the great truths in Your Word. But here I am complaining about several lost hours each day. Why can't I get these things together? Am I too lazy? Or have I grown accustomed to these lost hours and don't want to give them up?

Lord, let's talk again about those lost hours, and how to get a little joy from them. But I have to run now. The taxi driver wants his fare.

Thou wilt shew me the path of life: in thy presence is fulness of joy; at thy right hand there are pleasures for evermore.

Psalms 16:11

I Joy When You Hurt

Some weep when others weep, through sympathy.
Some laugh when others laugh, through fraternity.
Some weep when others laugh, through jealousy.
Some laugh when others weep, through revenge.
But I joy when you hurt.
Not always, only at times.
Not because I hate you,
But because I love you.
I joy when you hurt enough
To seek Someone who can change your life.
I joy when you turn away
From the sin that made you hurt,
And turn toward the only One
Who can wipe away all tears from your eyes.
I joy when you repent
And accept a completely new life in Him.
Do you see now
Why I found joy when you hurt?
It was for your eternal good.
Thorns for a moment.
Crowns forever.
That's the way Jesus hurt.
Is it wrong for us to hurt that way, too?

Joy Is. . . .

Error is the inevitable consequence of living.
Mutual error is the inevitable consequence of living
together.
Argument or faultfinding is the defensive mechanism to
preserve an ego in trouble.
Confession is the sacrifice of ego on the altar of love.
Forgiveness is the balm of healing that soothes and heals
the wounds of error.
Joy is the fresh new path, stretching out before the forgiver
and the forgiven.

No Deposit—No Return

It wasn't free. I'm sure of that. Nothing is.

But it's clearly marked on the outside. This thing has no further value. It has served its purpose. Please don't bother anyone else with it except the garbage collector.

That's not a very exciting role to fill. I mean, what would I think if I were that empty bottle? How would I feel? I carried whatever I carried to whomever wanted it. I did all I was asked to do. Now I'm rejected.

No deposit. No return.

They didn't even recognize my initial value. At least they could have said, "You really paid seven and one-half cents for me when you bought this product. But you aren't going to get it back because that's the way it is." I would have felt better, at least seven and one-half cents better.

I think I'll stop pretending to be the bottle. It makes me feel depressed. But I do feel sorry for it.

The manufacturer rejects it.

The bottler doesn't want it back.

The grocer lays no further claim to it.

I don't want to keep it around without a reason.

And the environmentalist curses it.

Nobody wants it, except to serve its purpose.

Wait!

Is that something I missed?

The bottle *was* important to the manufacturer. Wasn't it the source of his income, the reason for his being, the very foundation of his business? Without that bottle, he would disintegrate, fall apart at the seams.

And what about the bottler? How could he be a bottler without a bottle? No way! You can't ship soft drinks or syrup in paper cups. No. The bottle's the thing.

Do you think the grocer wants to sell lemon extract from a big drum? Or vinegar from a barrel? Hurrah for the bottle!

I certainly wouldn't want to go to the supermarket with pails and jars and jugs to do my shopping, would you? Think how my messy refrigerator would become that much more messy.

Bottle! I appreciate you! I appreciate your quiet service and I want to thank you for it.

Bottle! I see myself on the shelf with you at times. I see "no deposit—no return" stamped all over me. No one stands around me telling me how valuable I am to them. No, they just use my services and pass by to other things.

You and I could feel sorry for ourselves. I don't have seven and one-half cents stamped on me either. And when my service is concluded, I can't be ground up to try a recycled second chance.

But I won't feel sorry for myself. My Manufacturer had a purpose in mind for me. That's why He made me the way He did. So I'm going to do my best to fulfill that purpose. And while I'm doing it, I won't worry about "no return." I won't even worry about "no deposit," and the lack of value often placed upon me.

Instead, I'll rejoice that I can be a bottle, a real, live bottle, carrying the Water of Life to others. Because I'm doing the job I was made to do, I know that others will find joy in me.

If. . . .

If my life is preoccupied with getting, I will have too many things to permit room for joy.

If my life is burdened with worries and cares, I will crowd out that important guest called joy.

If my concern is building wealth alone, I will build a wall with no doors through which joy can enter.

If my interests are focused on building my own kingdom, I will never learn that joy comes through service to my King.

If my desires demand constant satisfaction, I may saturate myself until I have no appetite for true joy.

If my life requires me in the driver's seat at all times, I may miss the joy of divine guidance.

But . . .

If I make room for the Lord in my life, I open the way for the Lord to fill me with abundance of joy.

> Then will I go unto the altar of God, unto God my exceeding joy.
>
> Psalms 43:4

A Time to Punt

It's fourth down and ten yards to go.

Time to punt. No question about it.

There's a right time to run. Or pass. Or try for a field goal. But this is not the right time.

Does it ever seem like a team is quitting when it punts? Sometimes they do it with fourth and one. But it's not worth losing the game to risk getting that first down.

It's easy to sit on the sidelines and grumble when it's time to punt. "I'd like to get in there and show them how to do it."

If I did, I'd be mauled. This is no place for middle-aged men who play their football from a rocking chair.

Let them punt. Give up the ball at the right time. It may help them win the game.

Every winning team has to punt a few times in the game. It's all part of winning. They don't cave in when they have to do it. It's routine, like the bus driver who has to turn left to follow his route.

I wish I could remember this when I have to punt every now and then. To keep running with the ball is unwise and defeating. To punt seems like quitting. But it isn't. It's part of winning the game.

Now that helps! I'm glad that's settled.

But there's something else I must learn. It's not enough to punt. I have to punt like a winner—not like a loser. A loser punts with his chin down. A winner punts with his chin up.

Did you ever stop to think that there can be joy in punting? If I punt to win the game, I should discover joy in doing it. Or if I punt to win the victory over myself, even when I lose the game.

Lord, help me to accept the little defeats that lead me to the greater victory. Don't let me lie down and give up when each one comes along.

Lord, show me the joy of losing little things to gain the greater crown.

Teach me to lose my ego to gain Your love.

Help me lose my pride to gain Your "well done."

Show me how to give up gold to gain eternal riches.

Lead me through service to Your reward.

Teach me how to give up things to gain Your best.

Show me how to lose my sins to gain Your new life.

Help me to learn to punt when victory is at stake.

Lord, there is a time to give up the ball and let the other fellow run with it. Teach me wisdom to see that right time and punt.

Then give me the joy of celebrating victory, even when the scoreboard says I lost.

The Joy of Discipline

I prayed for joy,
    but He sent discipline
    that I might step in line with Him
    and follow in His steps
    until He leads me
    to the place of joy.

The Sliding Squirrel

I'm sure the squirrel didn't think it was funny.

But I did. Let me tell you how it happened.

In the summer, I had built the bird feeder and mounted it on a wood post outside our dining-room window. In my mind, I could see the winter birds holding their daily conventions there. With a $2.19 bag of seed, we could entertain ourselves and our bird friends for months.

But the birds didn't have a chance.

Winter hadn't come yet when a pesky squirrel discovered an easy meal. It was nothing for him to scamper up that wood post. Roosting on the pile of seeds, he scooped them up with a vengeance. What he didn't eat, he kicked out on the ground to be buried under the leaves and snow.

That squirrel and I drew our battle lines.

Chasing him away did nothing. He was back before I could get settled in my chair again. Hanging cans around the post offered him a little challenge, but it certainly didn't keep him out of my bird feeder.

There was only one thing to do. I mounted the bird feeder on a smooth iron pole. Let that squirrel try to climb a slippery pole!

I chuckled as I thought of those contests at the county fairs when I was a boy. Anyone who could climb to the top of a greased pole won a prize. Of course, he didn't have much time to enjoy it, for he had to spend the rest of the day cleaning the grease from his hands and burning his clothing.

I parked by the window and waited for the squirrel to come back. I didn't have to wait long, for he had become fat and greedy by now.

The new pole made him a little suspicious at first. But passion won out and he started up.

As I said, the squirrel didn't think it was nearly as funny as I did. He made it about a foot from the ground. Then he started to slide. Down he went with a bump.

On the next try, he made it almost to the top. But the pole was too much of a challenge and down he went.

Suddenly I identified with that squirrel. There! The fellow made it up about fifteen inches. That's when we had saved up a nice little nest egg. Then the old car gave out and we had to buy a new one. That's when the squirrel went back down to the ground with a bump.

This time he almost made it to the top. That's when we had almost paid off the house mortgage. But the slide back down to the bottom again reminded me how we had to open it up to pay for the big emergency that came.

Time after time he tried. But each time he went back down to the ground. I almost felt sorry for the squirrel . . . and myself.

I felt a little sad when the squirrel gave up at last and headed back to his normal diet of acorns. He walked that way, and I walked this way, headed for my chair.

"Lord, my life has been like that squirrel, up and down, up and down, on a greased pole. But please don't let me run away defeated."

Then I remembered. He is able "to keep you from falling, and to present you faultless before the presence of his glory with exceeding joy" (Jude 24). I have Someone with me to hold me up when I start to slide. I don't have to climb all alone. Not only will He keep me from falling, but He will lift me up into His glory with unlimited joy. The joy comes when He takes me to the top.

As I pondered this wonderful new truth, I scooped up a double handful of bird seed and dumped it at the foot of that squirrel's favorite tree. "Conscience money!" I thought. But it was fun to watch that squirrel feast without falling.

Take Love . . . and Get Joy, Too

If you accept God's love, you will permit Him to bear the fruit of joy in your life.

If you accept the love of His people, you will share in the joy that comes from knowing them.

If you share the love of God with others, you will also share the glad tidings of great joy.

If you share your love by sharing yourself, you will find joy in total giving.

Without love, there would have been no Creation, for God made a world and you to love and bring Him joy.

Without love, there would have been no angelic message at Bethlehem, for God sent His Son to bring good tidings of great joy to all people.

Without love, there would have been no Calvary, for God gave His love and His Son so that the world might know the joy of sins forgiven and heaven opened.

Without love, there would have been no Pentecost, for God sent His Spirit to minister to His people and help them know the joy of His presence with them day-by-day.

Without love, there would be no body of believers, for God has brought us together in His love so that we might share His joy and ours with one another.

Take love—God's love and the love of His people—and get joy, too!

New Friends From Old Books

Tonight I found a new friend.

Or should I say an old friend?

He would be about 175 years old now, if he were still living with us. But he isn't. He died long before I was born.

So, we never met.

It's a shame. I would like so much to have met with him, talked with him, probed his mind and heart to discover him.

Now I must be content with this old book which I bought at the resale shop. But it's his book. He wrote it during another era, in the midst of other circumstances, in a climate I never knew.

Through it, he spoke to me. He reached deep down inside my heart and touched me.

How could he?

He never heard my name. He never knew that I would be born, or that I would buy his book in a resale shop. I'm sure he would have written the same book and would have said the same things anyway. One reader a century later wouldn't change things that much.

I'll never be his friend on this earth. How could I? But he will be my friend, now that I've discovered him. I will treasure his friendship and cultivate it again and again as I read his book. I will keep a sharp eye for any other books that he has written. And I will buy them, even if they are not in a resale shop. I'll gladly pay full price or a premium price for them, for they will help me cultivate our one-way friendship. And I know he will never write another.

I can't help but think of our first face-to-face meeting when we finally get together in heaven.

"Hello, old friend," I'll say.

It will be fun to watch the blank stare on his face. "I . . . I don't believe we've met," he'll say.

Then I'll tell him about our one-way friendship, and how much I know about him and the work he did and the words he wrote. I'll even tell him how we met in a resale shop. He should get a chuckle from that!

I hope he will want to sit down for a year or two and cultivate a two-way friendship. I must remind him that I want this very much.

Oh, if you happen to be reading this book a hundred years after it was written, I'll be so glad that it still is speaking to people like you. And remember, too, that I want to be your friend.

It is the unknown, unseen friends like you that bring me joy. And it's also the old friends like him that bring me joy, too. Or is he a new friend?

Joy in Your Success

If I
    think about your success,
    plan for your success,
    pray for your success,
    genuinely hope for your success, and
    work for your success,
Then I will
    rejoice in your success.

Joy comes from
    involving myself in your life
    to the extent
    that you become an important part of mine.

Joy is . . . you, an essential part of me.

Colossians 2:5 tells me that even though I am physically far
away from you, I am with you in spirit, building my joy through
your successful living for Christ.

The Joy of Poverty

I prayed for joy,
  but He sent poverty
  that I might see my empty soul
  and reach out
  for Him to fill it
  with His gift of joy.

Can I Have Joy?

Can I have joy without loving the Prince of Joy and all
His friends?

Can I have joy without making peace with Him and all His
friends?

Can I have joy without faithfully following Him and
faithfully
serving all His friends?

Can I have joy without exercising the kindness and
goodness
which He has shared with me and all His friends?

Can I have joy without holding firm to the reins of life,
exercising the self-control in my relationships to Him
and all His friends?

Can I have joy without patiently waiting for the Lord to
work out His string of miracles in me?
These are the fruit of His spirit which He wants to
produce through me. Galatians 5:22 says the fruit of
the Spirit is love, joy, peace, patience, kindness,
goodness, faithfulness, gentleness, self-control.

The Lesson of the Raindrops

Lord, forgive me for grumbling about the rain.

But You know how difficult it is to commute to work in this stuff. I don't mind the wet feet as much as the honking horns and snarling drivers. Why is it that a little hot water in the tub makes a man feel like a king? But a little cold water on his car turns him into a dragon.

Before breakfast, I stole a little time to watch the rain make lazy designs on the window. The children joined me, and we made friends with some of the raindrops.

There! See this new one starting its trip at the top of the window? That's Edgar. Let's watch Edgar's travels. Oh. Oh. He just got into George's car and they are traveling down the window together. Now they pick up Frank . . . and drive down the window at a faster pace.

We wondered what George and Edgar and Frank were talking about as they made their trip down the windowpane. Were they discussing their morning flights in from some remote gray cloud?

"The wind was a little strong this morning. That made our landing rough."

Or were they complaining about their raindrop family? "Gladys was so grouchy this morning when I left. We had a few words, and . . . oh, well, we don't get along too well anyway."

"Maybe they're talking about us," one of the children volunteered. It was an interesting thought. I wondered what the raindrops would say if they could talk about us.

"I think they're talking about the beautiful things," another child said, interrupting my new thoughts.

"Like what?" I wondered.

"You know," she said. "Like the things you and your friends must talk about in the car. Like God and the things He does for you and what you can do for Him."

That hurt.

The truth is, we hadn't been talking about those things. We had been grumbling about the rain, or snow, or rush-hour traffic. We had been preoccupied with stock markets and gold prices and the problems in the Middle East.

No, we really hadn't been talking about the important things.

Later that morning, the fellows thought I had lost my grip on life when I pointed to the windshield of the car and said, "Do you see Edgar sliding down? Let me tell you what he's saying to Frank."

It took me a while to convince them that I really hadn't been working too hard and needed a rest. Then they saw it. We had missed the joy of the Lord because we had not been rejoicing in the Lord. Isn't that what He said we should do? "Rejoice in the Lord alway: and again I say, Rejoice" (Philippians 4:4).

Strange. We didn't grumble about the rain. We just rejoiced in the lesson of the raindrops.

The Two-Minute Warning

Have you ever noticed?

They always start to play football at the two-minute warning. Oh, they play well before that. But something happens when the two-minute warning sounds.

Especially to losers. I've seen teams play more football in the last two minutes than during the whole second quarter.

Have you noticed? Have you wondered why?

Why do we adjust our expenses to our incomes?

Why do we get up in the morning so that we will be just barely on time, or just barely late for work? Or for Sunday school?

Why do we leave the house on a schedule that makes us drive like maniacs? Five minutes more would have worked wonders.

Have you ever noticed how much more we get done when we *have* to do it? When our backs are up against the wall? The two-minute warning has sounded and we jump to attention and start moving.

Lord, help me to blow the whistle ten minutes earlier. Help me to get up and get moving while there's still time to do something about it. Help me to sleep when I've won the victory, and not until.

This game called life has so much more at stake than the game called football. Lord, help me play the game for what it is. That scoreboard keeps flashing for a long, long, long time after the game is over.

The two-minute warning has sounded. Now I hope I have more than two minutes to do my best.

If I do my best before I *have* to, I'll get a lot more joy from it. Lord, You know how much I want that joy, and need it. So . . . blow that whistle loud and clear. Now! Please?

The Joy of Reunion

I have a big, empty place in my heart for you. I'll never forget your tears when we parted. When we do get together, my emptiness will be filled with joy (*see* 2 Timothy 1:4).

There were once two couples.

"For crying out loud, Sarah, isn't dinner ready yet? I'm going to be late for bowling."

That was Tom, rushing in from work.

Tom and Sarah had reunion. But no tears of joy. Just tears. And angry words.

"Where's my little kitten?" That's Russ, coming home from work. "Ummmm." That's Sue, sharing the joy with Russ of thirty seconds in each other's arms. They're preoccupied with each other. Not bowling. Not dinner. Not the problems of the day. Just each other.

That's the joy of being together again. Even though it was just eight and one-half hours ago that they parted.

There were once two couples . . . yours and ours. But what are we like when it's time for this kind of joy?

Watering the Seeds of Joy

It isn't easy for a father to spank his little girl. He seems so big. She seems so little. And innocent, even when it's obvious that she isn't.

There was a time, one of many, when it had to be done. In a very ungirllike fit of temper, she had bitten her younger sister on the arm and had drawn blood.

As I say, it's never easy for a father to spank his little girl, even though she has acted like a cannibal. The old saying that it hurts me more than you is painfully true at such a time. But I had to do it and I did it.

There were tears. This was no time to conserve water. The way she cried told me that her pride and vanity hurt more than the backside of her anatomy.

I almost shed a few myself. She was standing in the corner, covering her wounds, and dignity, with her two little hands.

When the tears and sobs quieted a little, I asked softly, "Do you know why I had to spank you?"

"Yes."

"Have you learned something from this?"

"Yes."

"What?"

"That you don't love me anymore!" More tears.

"But have you learned something that you should never do again?"

"Yes."

"What?"

"But she hit me first."

The lesson wasn't coming through very fast. I tried the same line of questions until she "confessed" what I wanted to hear. She would never, never bite her little sister again.

At least, not until the next time.

But the lesson was only half over. I could have left and let her cry it out. That is, I think I could. But I didn't.

"Do you love me?". I asked cautiously.

"Yes."

"Would you like to come into my arms and love me?"

That was all that she needed. She flew into my arms and sobbed out her hurt until it was all over.

We sat there for some time. She was snuggled up against me, seeking comfort from the very person who had wounded her.

At last, like the coming of morning, her smile began to play on her little face. Then her eyes twinkled. As I held her close, she kissed me like some long-lost cousin.

"I love you, Daddy," she whispered.

She must have wondered why I was so quiet, but I had to catch up on some praying.

"Lord," I said silently, "help me to be as wise as this little girl. When You spank me, give me the good sense to run right into Your arms and tell You how much I love You."

As I watched the smile on her face, I knew that my Father had taught me a lesson about joy that I would never forget. ". . . weeping may endure for a night, but joy cometh in the morning" (Psalms 30:5). The seeds of joy are often watered with my tears. Lord, help me to discover the joy that comes from Your correction, the joy in recognizing how much You love me.

Strength

Lord, You know that men aren't supposed to be weak. Nobody likes a weak fellow. He can pick up so many unwanted names. Sissy! Fem! Runt! These words can pierce a young boy's mind like a sword.

You know how we are taught from childhood to be strong men. Sometimes we have to fight to prove it and get bloody noses. Even when we're older, we have to keep on fighting for our identity as strong men, but now we use other devices instead of our fists.

I think of the strong men in the Bible, Lord. You seemed to love them. There was David, and Moses, and Gideon, and Samson. They could have all starred in Westerns. Are those the men after Your own heart?

But, Lord, I just thought of some other names, too. I don't think Joseph ever held a sword in his hand. He never needed to. And what about the Apostle John? He certainly was no warrior. Why did You love these men, Lord? What did You see in them?

Lord, if I don't stand up as a strong man, will the world run over me, stamp me into the ground, take what I have, and discard me on the heap with other weak men? You wouldn't want that to happen to me, would You?

When I was a boy, Lord, I was taught that strong men don't cry. But I've seen tears in the eyes of men who could mop up the floor with me. Men don't cry, but these did. I think they had encountered something that couldn't be licked with big biceps. Like a disrupted marriage, or a child who rejected them, or the death of a loved one.

It's a strange feeling, Lord, when men like that come to ask for strength. Strength? I wouldn't last ninety seconds in the ring with them. What do they want?

Could I have some strength that brawny men need?

What is this, Lord?

". . . the joy of the Lord is your strength!" That's what it says in Nehemiah 8:10. When strong men come to ask for strength, is this what they want? Lord, have they discovered something in me that I was not aware was showing?

I guess some must have detected how delighted I am to belong to You, Lord. It's not that I'm so strong. No, it's just that I'm so happy that I have a strong God to take care of me. I'm so glad that Your joy is my joy. That's worth more than a tough guy's chin or a boxer's muscles in the time of trouble.

Thank You, Lord, for sending Your joy to make me strong. I would be so weak without it.

The Joy of Obedience

To obey a fool is foolish.
To obey a stranger is irresponsible.
To obey an enemy is self-destructive.
To obey your own desires is carnal.
To obey Satan is sin.
To obey the Lord of Life is both wisdom and joy.

Romans 7:22 tells me that deep down inside I
will find joy in doing what God has told me to do.

The Joy Tree

Was that nice, Lord?

I mean, calling me a tree? I really don't know if You intended that as a compliment or a challenge.

There's the old tree by the back fence. One good storm and it will come down, taking the fence with it. The squirrels and birds seem to know about it. They pass it up for stronger trees nearby. No, surely You didn't mean that.

What about the thorn tree by the swamp? The children don't climb that one. There has never been a child's laughter from its branches. No, we leave it alone and it leaves us alone. When the children list their "fun" trees, they pass it by like poison.

I hope You weren't talking about that little seedling we planted last spring. We call that our fifty-fifty tree. It has a 50 percent chance of succeeding and a 50 percent chance of not making it through the year. I don't have many ambitions to be like that tree.

Lord, let me read it again. You may help me discover some clue as to the tree You want me to be.

"And he shall be like a tree planted by the rivers of water, that bringeth forth his fruit in his season; his leaf also shall not wither; and whatsoever he doeth shall prosper" (Psalms 1:3).

Of course, Lord, how thoughtless of me! I forgot the orchard! But how could I? It's a favorite family place in season. There's not a person in our family who turns up his nose at our lovely fruit trees.

Last spring we almost moved into the orchard when the buds burst into full bloom. How can You make such beautiful blooms and such sweet perfume come from old dead-looking twigs, Lord? I don't understand it. But I love it. We all do.

You know how much the children enjoy watching the fruit grow. From fragrant blossom to delicious fruit. All in one summer. How *do* You do it, Lord?

So, don't let me forget the orchard, Lord. Don't let me forget the miracle of the fruit and the pleasure of eating it.

Did You have that in mind when You mentioned, "The fruit of the Spirit?" What was it now? Love, joy, peace, patience, kindness, goodness, faithfulness, gentleness, self-control. What a wonderful fruit bowl! Are You trying to tell me that I can be the kind of tree that bears all that fruit? I'm almost afraid to claim that promise, Lord. It's so big!

But wait! I almost missed something again. You didn't say that this is *my* fruit, did You? You said it is the fruit of Your Spirit in me. I think I see it now, Lord. You just want to be fruitful through me.

I can't argue about that. If You want me in Your orchard, I'll be Your kind of tree, Lord. And thank You for asking.

Suffering . . . and Joy

I prayed for joy,
     but He sent suffering
     and drove me to the suffering Saviour
     who knew the Cross,
     the gateway
     to the crown of joy.

The Joy of Wealth, the Wealth of Joy

Wealth is not how much I own,
But how much I share.
Merely to possess is poverty,
For it imprisons my resources
And forbids them service.
It is in making others richer
That I discover the joy of wealth,
And the wealth of joy.
What wealth do I value most?
Would I sell my eyesight
For a ton of pure gold?
Would I put a price tag of a million dollars
On each of my children?
Would I sell my soul
For a carload of diamonds?
Or a room full of one thousand dollar bills?
Would I accept all the money
In the world's largest bank
To never hear a note of music
Or the sound of a human voice again?
How many green stamps would I take
To isolate myself from all my friends
For the rest of my life?
How many stocks and bonds would I accept
To cut off the name of Jesus
From my vocabulary,
Or the Word of God
From my sight?

To have good eyesight
May make me happy,
But to use good eyesight to read God's Word
Will bring me joy.

To have children
May make me happy,
But to lead those children in God's ways
Will bring me joy.

To have good health and strength
May make me happy,
But to exercise that strength in God's service
Will bring me joy.

To have good friends
May make me happy,
But to share God's riches with them
Will bring me joy.

To own a Bible and know it's there
May make me happy,
But to read it, understand it, live it, and share it
Will bring me joy.

True wealth is sharing God's treasures,
And this is joy.

The Brown Christmas Tree

I was startled when I saw it.

A *brown* Christmas tree! No ornaments. No garlands or tinsel, and no bright lights.

Of course, there was a reason. This was not December. It was February.

Since we live in the country, we have to dispose of our own tree. There are no community tree-burnings. No curbside pickup. We do have a garbage truck that grinds its way into our place weekly, devouring things that have grown too ugly or too plenteous for us to keep.

It has always seemed a sacrilege to throw a Christmas tree into the dragon's jaws. So we put aside the inevitable and lay it on a brush pile in the back, waiting for spring to come. Later, fallen limbs and persistent leaves join it in the fires of spring-cleaning.

I would argue with you all day about the pollution from that tree. To me it's like a sweet smelling aroma of some ancient sacrifice.

But, standing there with the cold February winds pulling at my coat, I was drenched in my thoughts of the tree. It was so alone and out of place. It wasn't the lively green of a Christmas tree, but the ugly brown of transition—somewhere between yesterday's green and tomorrow's total surrender.

I stood silently with the tree for a while. Once more the sights and sounds of Christmas swept over me, seemingly coming forth from the branches that had heard and seen so much in that short time.

The laughter and shouts of children as they opened gifts on Christmas morning.

The voices of friends coming through the door, offering

courteous words about the tree, stamping snow from their shoes, and mingling their joys with ours in being together.

The sounds of great choirs and orchestras, brought into our home for a command performance on a plastic disc.

The aroma of cookies baking in the oven.

The quiet, hushed voices of our family, sitting around the tree on Christmas eve, reading the Story of Stories from His Word about His coming, and talking about the true meaning and joys of this most wonderful time.

We had cut this tree ourselves in mid-December at a place that grew it for that purpose. With laughter and bright hope, we mounted it in a stand and hung ornaments and garlands on its branches. The tree had brought us together into an experience of delight and we would think of it often.

Now, it is no more than an unwanted semibrown piece of trash, waiting to be burned in spring-cleaning. Or is it?

Tomorrow this tree will be gone, a pile of ashes to blow away on a careless wind. Scattered into nearby fields and prairies, it will go down into anonymity, to be forgotten. Or will it?

I often think of trees of Christmases past. I remember certain trees of childhood. Sometimes we resurrect pictures of bygone Christmases and talk of happy times we shared beneath some tree which has long since returned to the soil from which it grew. And we remember that tree with gladness and great joy. Without it, that Christmas would never have been what it was.

Old friend, I do remember you with joy. You may be yesterday's Christmas tree. Or you may be a senior friend who helped me along life's early road. But I have not forgotten you. And when I remember, I remember you with great joy in my heart. I will never forget. I want you to know that. I will always remember you with great joy.

Appointments

Lord, my appointment book is bulging.

There is a luncheon on Tuesday, crowded in between a half dozen or so business appointments during the day. After dinner, I'm scheduled to be at PTA.

It's the same thing on Wednesday, and Thursday, and the other days. Just the names change.

How does this happen, Lord? Why do we get so busy with our activities and fill up our appointment books like this?

Today I had a minute to think. That's unusual. A real luxury! You know that, Lord.

I thought about my appointment book. I looked at the names in it.

Then I felt ashamed. I couldn't find some very important names. The real VIPs in my life.

Where was my wife's name? I didn't have her down for 3:30 Wednesday afternoon, or luncheon on Monday, or an evening of fun and relaxation. No, her name should be up there near the top of the list.

There are some other VIPs I missed. My children. Where are they scheduled? They need my time just as much as these other names do. More! Much more! I can see that I need to rework my book and get things in better order.

Oh, how could I forget, Lord? I don't have You in here either. Look at all those other names and dates and places! Not once do I have Your name down for a specific time and place.

"Meet God at the family-room chair at 7:30 A.M. Purpose of meeting: straighten out priorities. Rearrange appointments, and make sure VIPs are put in top place."

Lord, help me rearrange my appointments the way they should be.

Joy is putting things in the right perspective.

The Gift of Joy

I prayed for joy,
        but He sent trials and temptations
        to stretch and bend
        and build my patience
        without which
        there could be no gift of joy.

All the Family Rejoices

The trip was off. There was no way that we would take it now. Later, perhaps. But not now.

One child was sick. Everyone else was perfectly healthy and ready to go. But not one member of the family would leave on that trip until everyone could go. It was an act of unity not seen in daily life.

Children can fight together, argue together, call each other names, and otherwise try to discredit one another at home. But if one is threatened on the outside, or if one suffers from outside influences, the whole family unifies suddenly.

"We'll wait until everyone is well and can go," I volunteered. There was not one dissenting vote. Of course, we weren't really voting anyway. But sometimes it's nice to vote in such a way that everyone thinks we could be voting, even though we're not. You know what I mean, don't you?

We had discovered the taste of 1 Corinthians 12:26, "And whether one member suffer, all the members suffer with it." That's the first part. We were to discover the second part not long after, "or one member be honoured, all the members rejoice with it."

Our oldest daughter had practiced for weeks to play a senior solo in the final high-school orchestra concert. It was an exciting affair. A national music figure was guest conductor for some of the numbers. The local civic auditorium was filled. Parents were there; school leaders were there. And we were there! All of us.

When it came time for her solo, our graduating senior outdid herself. She had mastered her number, and for her age, her instrument. The applause showed clearly that she had convinced the audience of her skills.

It is at times like these that every father and mother would like to wear a six-inch celluloid button which says, "I am her father," or "I am her mother." We'd like to stand up and take a bow, too.

"That's our daughter," we would shout to the whole audience. "She's ours. Did you hear? If not, we can shout louder."

Of course we can't do things like that. If for no other reason, we might embarrass our daughter.

But after the concert, we all basked in her glory.

"My, *your* daughter did so well," someone said.

"Your daughter really made a hit tonight," said another.

Even her brothers enjoyed the honors.

"Your sister certainly knows how to play!"

I think we weren't really proud of ourselves. No, how could we be? We hadn't done anything. We were just glad that she was part of our family. Or, should I say that we were part of her family. It was *her* night.

"Or one member be honoured, all the members rejoice with it."

The joy of success was hers that night. But it was ours, too. We rejoiced because she rejoiced, just as we would have suffered if she had been suffering.

You know that. You've suffered with your child.

You've rejoiced with your child.

The joy of one member of the family becomes the joy of all.

Don't you think it's the same in God's family?

When I Am Weak

I cannot always be
A pinnacle of strength.
Sometimes I will be
A blob of weakness.
The question is not
Whether I will be weak.
The question is:
What I will do
When I find that I am?
Will I give up?
Will I feel sorry for myself?
Will I give in to forces
That come to possess me?
Will I submit
To depression,
And fall prey
To further weakness?
Will I try to fight
In my own weak strength?
Or will I seek Someone
With unlimited strength,
Waiting to send
An abundant supply?
Will I recognize that,
When I am weak,
He is strong?
My extremity
Is His opportunity.
My deficiency
Is His sufficiency.

My need
Is His supply.
But I must seek Him,
Ask Him,
And let Him supply
My every need.
Then I will know
The abundance of His joy.

Springtime Joy

This morning the sun is smiling.

I'm glad.

I'm tired of watching trees reach a thousand bony fingers toward slate gray skies. They look so much more friendly clothed in green, offering shade on a summer day.

Yes, this is all long overdue.

Even the clouds seem to be chasing each other eastward toward oblivion. They hurry, and in my mind, I encourage them to hurry faster. Behind them, a patchwork of blue emerges and with it a brighter hope.

Something tells me that it is time to put away the snow shovel. That awful necessity gave me many an aching back this year. I'm glad to hang it in some remote dusty corner of our overcrowded garage.

Does this mean that we can say good-bye to salt-strewn roads, glazed with ice and ridged with frozen snow? Is this the end of snowplows that interrupt the stillness of the early morning?

I certainly hope so.

I long for the first green shoot to appear in the daffodil bed. Then I know that the colors of spring will not be far behind.

The sun's smile is a warm, gentle, friendly smile.

The icicles are afraid of it. Amidst their tears, they shrink away. Only yesterday, they grew longer with the steady rhythmic dripping of the melting snow from the roof. They seemed to compete with one another to see which could grow longest by sunset.

But today? That's a different matter. They run with a steady stream. No time now to compete for growth. They struggle in a losing battle for survival.

Underfoot, melting snow has turned the ground into an oversaturated sponge. Little rivulets move in search of companions for a long journey. How I wish I could follow their course through tiny streams and great rivers, past farms and cities and out into an endless sea. What sights I would behold!

The spring thaw has reached beyond my sight and feel and melts my heart. It, too, seemed locked in winter's cold embrace.

There is nothing like a cold heart to freeze everything and everyone around me. Is it possible that, in the winter season of my heart, I have frozen out some soul seeking refuge? Is it possible that my cold indifference to others could have snuffed the warm light from my window and caused some traveler on the way of life to turn aside for counsel elsewhere?

Lord, forgive!

Lord, turn my heart into a smiling sun. Melt any patches of ice that yet remain. May Your joy not be put into a Deepfreeze in my own heart, preserved but not shared. For it is in sharing that joy that my own heart melts and causes the sunshine of Your face to shine upon me. In radiating Your joy, may I feel its smile bringing springtime into my heart.

What I Have and Lack

I do not always have
What I think I have.
I do not always lack
What I think I lack.
The lack of money is not true poverty.
If I lack money
But have the riches of God,
I am rich,
Not poor.
The lack of honor is not true shame.
If I lack the honor
Others can give,
But have the Lord's approval,
I am highly favored.
The lack of happiness
Is not joylessness.
If I lack the happiness
That comes from things going my way,
But have the assurance
Of the Lord's presence,
I have true joy.
No man desires poverty—
Economically or spiritually.
No man desires a lack of honor—
Among men or God.
No man desires unhappiness—
Or joylessness.
But there are times when poverty comes
As an unwanted guest.
There are times when men

Withhold honor from me.
And there are times when I will not know
The happiness of things going my way.
Joy is the result
Of the way I respond
To these situations.
If economic poverty is an excuse
For me to turn away from God,
Then I will be eternally poor.
But if it is the motivation
For me to seek the Lord's riches,
Then I will know wealth
Here and in the hereafter.
And I will know
The joy of the Lord,
For joy is knowing that I know Him,
No matter what I think I have
Or what I think I lack.

The Old Well

I often think of the old well.

As a boy, growing up on a midwestern farm, it caused mixed emotions in me. If you, too, grew up on a farm, you will sympathize.

There were times when the old well became Samson's prison. Have you ever pumped a hundred-gallon tank of water with an old cast-iron pump? Every few days, we attached the long pipe that led to this open tank and pumped until it was filled. That was the watering hole for horses and cows.

Of course it had to be done! The animals couldn't pump the water themselves. They were totally dependent on us to do it.

We had no plumbing inside the old farmhouse at first, so the well was everything. It was the source of drinking water, cooking water, bath water, wash water, and just plain water for a dozen other uses.

Secretly, we all feared long, dry seasons, for ours was a shallow well. It was also the only well. Without it, life would become unbearable.

But there were happy times associated with that well. How can I forget the dozens of colorful butterflies that gathered in the little pool of water that collected along the ground by the lowest corner of the concrete cover in which the pump was mounted. Our wasted water became their convention hall, where they gathered to refresh themselves before moving on across the broad, flat fields.

No soft drink or ice-cream cone ever refreshed me more than a drink of that cold water drawn from deep under the ground. Today, after becoming accustomed to "city water," it tastes like the iron pump that brings it up. But after a long hike with my dog, or working in the garden, or a trip into town, there was nothing more refreshing than that water from the old well.

To a hot, tired boy on a summer afternoon, the old well was *the* place to go.

Oh, the joy of drinking its cold, refreshing water! Suddenly life seemed new and fresh. A good, cold cup of water and I was ready to go again.

I remember something like this that the Lord said. "Therefore with joy shall ye draw water out of the wells of salvation" (Isaiah 12:3).

To the tired and thirsty, the weary and worn, what a wonderful message. When life gets hot and uncomfortable, where else can I find such deep refreshing joy? Is it little wonder that I want to rush to His wellsprings of joy?

Drink deep, soul, and you will be refreshed. Refuse, and you will always be thirsty.

The Joy of Tears

I prayed for joy,
    but He made me hurt and cry
    and made me watch others in pain
    until I ran to find a shelter
    under the One
    who heals us with His joy.

Why Do I Feel the Way I Do?

I'm sorry, but that is the way I feel.

I really don't want to, but I do. It happened by default. My own default. I was just too busy to do what I knew that I should do.

My youngest girl had been asking me for weeks to fix the stairs in her doll house. I want to. I really do. But I've been "too busy."

It's amazing how understanding a little child can be. More than adults, sometimes.

Last night I reminded her that I had not forgotten. It was just that I had been "too busy."

She smiled sweetly, put her arms around me and said softly, "I know. Mommy has told me that, too. I'll wait."

She's only seven.

Somehow it's really more than I deserve from a seven-year-old girl. I might have felt better if she had said, "Look. I'm tired of waiting. You've been putting me off for weeks now. What's more important, me or that stuff you're working on?"

If she had said it, I might have been angry. Maybe just plain mad. But I would have deserved it. And I would have tried to understand. It should be easier for a fellow in his forties to understand than a little girl who is seven. Shouldn't it?

What she said made me feel a little guilty.

Later, when I kissed her good night, she looked up at me with her big brown eyes and smiled a captivating little smile. Her eyes twinkled in the semidarkness.

"I love you," she whispered. "I'm so glad you're my daddy. We have fun together, don't we?"

That's true. We do.

But it just made me feel more guilty. We could have had

more fun if I had done the one thing she wanted so much.

Or could we?

Was this a growing experience for her to understand some of my problems?

I shouldn't feel guilty about that.

And was this a growing experience for me to realize that my seven-year-old was growing in a way that I might have missed?

I shouldn't feel guilty about that, either.

Now I felt a little confused. What I was doing wasn't right because it denied her of what she wanted. But it wasn't wrong because I really was too busy to do it now. I felt guilty because she was so sweet about it, but then I felt good because she was showing how much she was growing and developing an understanding.

Lord, why do I feel the way I do? Help me to know how I should feel.

I feel insufficient to handle some of these human problems by myself. What can You do for me, Lord?

Then I remembered. ''The joy of the Lord is your strength'' (Nehemiah 8:10).

When I am weak, insufficient, burdened with guilt, and confused, I need to appropriate the joy of the Lord into my life. That's what will make me stronger and wiser and less confused.

Why do I feel the way I do? Perhaps it's because I am me. But in Him, I will find a new strength, and a new joy.

Sunrise

It had been one of those mornings.

Everything happened. The alarm rang, but I didn't hear it. Really! I didn't! It could have been a two-ton truck driving into bed with me, and I still would not have heard it. That's what happens from staying up too late.

So all the routines started a few minutes later than I had planned. This was not funny, either. I had a breakfast flight to catch and I couldn't miss it.

It must have been like a three-ring comedy for my wife to watch me pull everything together. But she was polite and didn't laugh at all the stupid things that I can do under pressure. Perhaps it was because we had too many other things to talk about.

We had to get some little details covered about school vacations, whether or not we could go to PTA the night I would get back, whether we might have to borrow some money to pay the next mortgage payment or whether we could slide by if we didn't repair the car until the next month.

That wasn't all. I still hadn't fixed the leak in the corner of the roof and what should a woman do if we had an east rain while I was gone?

We didn't know whether to kiss good-bye or sign a mutual agreement of idiocy. We decided on the first and I headed for the airport, wondering what the rush-hour traffic would be like at such an unearthly hour. In my rush to get dressed and packed, I hadn't noticed that the whole out-of-doors was a big, gigantic glob of fog.

That hadn't been part of my travel plans.

Would the plane leave?

Would I be able to get to the airport on time in this stuff?

Traffic wasn't impossible. Just an unhealthy challenge. Enough to make me want to go back to more primitive ways of living. The cave man didn't have to jet somewhere before breakfast, and he survived. What did I have that he didn't? I was almost ready to trade.

Parking places were at a premium at the airport, but I finally managed to find one at the far end of the lot. No time to lose, though. I grabbed my bag, jumped out the door and ran down the parking lot toward the terminal.

Lights!

I had forgotten to turn them off.

Back I ran.

Two steps away from the car I remembered that I hadn't locked the thing. Back again.

Hold everything! Just wait a minute! Have I remembered all that I should before rushing off toward the terminal again?

Bag? Yes.

Lights? Yes.

Lock the car? Yes.

Ticket? Ticket! I grabbed for my inside coat pocket. Yes. I *had* put it there last night. Good thinking, Dum-Dum. Now, let's get going for the terminal, or I'll be spending the rest of the day waiting for another flight.

It was still dark and foggy as I ran into the terminal. I found the escalator, raced up to the counter, and deposited my ticket and bag.

I sensed a little pity in the eyes of the girl at the counter. But she had been taught to be polite.

"We don't have time to check your bag, sir," she said. "The flight is leaving on time. Your gate is F–11. Take your bag with you."

F–11? That's halfway home!

But I picked up my bag and ticket, now folded, punched, and otherwise mutilated to make it valid and headed for F–11.

Security check! How long would that take?

It went well and I struggled through in a few minutes.

Time was short, so I half-walked and half-ran to F–11. My ticket was collected, my seat assigned, and I stumbled on board, slid my bag under the seat, and collapsed next to a window.

That was close! The motors were already going and the doors were closing. I just made it.

We taxied through the fog to the runway. After waiting for two planes ahead of us, we headed up through the early morning fog.

I watched with a sense of awe as we swept up through the dense fog, or clouds. It was hard to tell the difference up here. It grew lighter and lighter as we went up.

Then suddenly the whole world changed in an instant of time. We burst from the clouds like a fish jumping out of the water.

Below, the world became a sea of rose-colored cotton, tinted with golds, yellows, oranges, blues, and purples. A rainbow must have burst and spilled its paintpots over the whole earth. At the far eastern end there was an iridescent pot of melted gold called the sun, rising up out of this rainbow sea and kissing the top of each cloud from one horizon to another.

It was really too beautiful to describe.

I sat there stunned and awed by this miracle of sight.

Then I suddenly realized. Below this rainbow sea, people were rushing to get to the airport, gulping down breakfast, racing somewhere in the fog, making last minute calculations with husband or wife and acting out the role of overworked humans.

Idiots! If you could just be here!

Nothing in that foggy, earthbound mess mattered at the moment. Nothing around me mattered. I didn't care if breakfast would be served or not. I was raptured, caught up into another world, where PTA and mortgages and car repairs didn't matter.

Lord, I whispered, is this what it will be like when You take me up on that final flight from earth? Will I look down at my previous days and say, "Idiot!"

I settled back in my seat. All the tension dropped away, and I feasted on the Lord and His bountiful beauty. I drenched my soul in the beauty of His presence and I knew His joy.

Joy and Prayer

I prayed for joy,
    but He asked me
    to pray for those with needs,
    that in bringing God and them together,
    I might find the joy
    of being included, too.

Sacrifices of Joy

Lord, let's talk about that word.

Whenever I hear about sacrifices, I think of people, long ago, hacking up animals and burning them. Is this what the word is all about?

But here it is, talking about something much different. ". . . therefore will I offer in his tabernacle sacrifices of joy" (Psalms 27:6).

That doesn't sound like animal sacrifice, Lord. Was there another kind, even then? Has there always been something else You wanted? Is this a sacrifice I should make today?

I like the idea of a sacrifice of joy, but I wouldn't want to burn my joy on an altar. Surely You didn't mean that, did You? Or did You mean that I should offer up my joy as a living sacrifice? Live it out. Let it radiate Your presence to others. Let it burn like fire into the lives of those around me. Would that be a worthy sacrifice of joy, Lord?

Now if I gave myself and my substance to You, wouldn't that be an offering with joy? That is, if I did it joyfully? Lord, spare me from giving grudgingly, for I just know that would not be an offering of joy.

What about the times I go to church, Lord? I'll have to ask myself if they were offerings of joy. Sometimes they weren't. Forgive me. I didn't mean to go grudgingly.

I suppose if I sing songs to You, or pray to You, or give to You, or work for You, I should do these things with joy. If I don't do my part with joy, can I expect You to send joy with Yours?

Lord, help me to learn the joy of giving as well as the joy of receiving.

Teach me to learn the joy of working as well as the joy of

having others do things for me.

Help me know the joy of going to Your house without dragging my feet, of listening to sermons without letting my mind wander, and doing my part in supporting Your house without thinking of the other things that money would buy.

Lord, teach me the joy of sacrifice and the sacrifice of joy.

Servitude

I prayed for joy,
    but He sent servitude,
    so that in serving Him and others
    I might know
    how He brought joy
    to those He loved.

A Worn-Out Bear

There's nothing glorious about carrying out the trash. I've never enjoyed it. I never will.

But once in a while there is a note of joy. Like the last trip I made from house to garage with a pail filled with trash.

Ordinarily I don't take inventory of all the unwanted things in the trash pail. There's not a very bright future in such exercises.

But in this case, I couldn't help but notice this creature, sticking its head above the other goodies, smiling at me with that pasted-on smile that had been there for the last fifteen years.

It was Chi-Chi, a very worn-out bear. What time and hours of play had not accomplished, some thoughtless mouse had. It was time to retire Chi-Chi from active service.

Our oldest daughter would never have done this without some encouragement from her mother. In the heat of housecleaning, Chi-Chi had to go.

But I felt an inner struggle carrying that smiling face out, for I remembered the times he had figured in our family memories.

Chi-Chi first appeared fifteen years earlier to comfort a little girl who had just lost her tonsils. We had waited in her hospital room with Chi-Chi and prayed for her safety. And for the doctor who was so important to her at that moment.

Later, as she came out from under the ether, she looked around the room. She smiled, then saw Chi-Chi and reached out for him. From that moment, he became her companion during her recuperation.

Chi-Chi had brought joy to her, but her joy had brought a greater joy to us. Chi-Chi was a friend in the time of suffering, and that suffering brought us all together with a sense of joy.

Oh, there was another time when we had a little discipline problem. For a moment, our little girl turned into a monster and threw Chi-Chi across the room, knocking down a favorite vase and sending it on its way to the city dump.

We laugh with her about such times now. And we cried with her about them then. But even the memory of discipline brings back a sense of joy, for it was in discipline that we helped her grow to be the strong, faithful woman of God that she is today. Chi-Chi was an instrument of that joy which came out of discipline.

Chi-Chi's downfall came from an act of kindness and generosity. It was a matter last year of another little girl wanting what her older sister had.

"If you take care of my Chi-Chi," was the condition, "I'll let you play with him."

But little girls don't always take care of things that aren't theirs. Our littlest girl was no exception.

Chi-Chi fell into hard times. He was clothed, fed, scrubbed, and otherwise mutilated. It wasn't surprising that he began to come apart at the seams.

His final days came in a box of discarded toys in an out-of-the-way back closet. As I said, some thoughtless mouse decided that he would make excellent building materials for a mouse house.

So he was discovered, beyond hope, by our eldest daughter. There were tears, but he was beyond surgery.

An era had come to an end, and it was my lot to take him to his semifinal resting place.

I dumped him unceremoniously into the big trash cans by the garage and made my way back toward the house, still filled with memories, not so much of Chi-Chi, but of "his" girl who had brought so much joy to our house. And I thanked God for every remembrance of her.

I suppose she thought I had lost touch with life, but I

couldn't help throwing my arms around her. "I'm glad for all the joy you've brought us," I whispered. "Thank you."

"What brought this on?" she said with a laugh.

"Chi-Chi."

"Oh."

I knew she understood.

Then we talked for a long time about the mutual joy of parent and child, of good times and the not-so-good. It's strange what a mouse-eaten worn-out bear can do. But Chi-Chi brought back a prayer into our hearts and memories of earlier joys. And he reminded us of joys that are now, and that will be for years to come.

Thanks, Chi-Chi. We needed your last reminder.

A reminder of joy!

Think of Philemon

In Philemon 7, Paul told Philemon that: Your love has brought me much joy and comfort, my brother, because the kindness you have shared with God's people has done so much for them.

The next time you are tempted to give a check *instead* of yourself, think of Philemon.

The next time you are tempted to give your mate security *instead* of your own love and attention, think of Philemon.

The next time you are tempted to give your own children things *instead* of yourself, think of Philemon.

The next time you are tempted to pray for God's people *instead* of prayerfully involving yourself in their needs, think of Philemon.

The next time you are tempted to give the Lord your best intentions *instead* of yourself, think of Philemon.

It was Philemon's personal love and kindness that brought joy. Joy is . . . *YOU,* prayerfully and generously involved in my life.

Trophies

It's that time of year again in our community. You know, basketball fever.

It's something like football fever, but the germ is a different species. It strikes during the winter season instead of the fall.

But it hits hard. The symptoms are terrifying. It turns mothers into screaming creatures that are very unlike mothers. And fathers become dragons, breathing out fire at innocent high-school boys from another town.

The gladiators would have been proud of an audience like that!

I've often wondered how a Martian would analyze this sport if he stumbled onto a basketball floor immediately after landing. How would he report it to his superiors back home?

"There were five earthlings in their strange, bright underclothes. They fought five other earthlings, trying to get a sphere to one end of a big room, so they could throw it away into a net. Then they all ran to the other end of the room while the five other earthlings tried to throw it away into their net. Around them, crowds of earthlings screamed and shouted."

Why do people go through such exercises? Why do young men spend long afternoons exerting themselves to the limit?

I could make a list of many personal values such as exercise, team spirit, sportsmanship, and others. But in our state, the climax is called The Sweet Sixteen, or the state championship. If a team is good enough, that's what it works for.

Unless you've followed a team into a state championship, you can't imagine the feverish pitch that builds. What wouldn't a team give to get into that tournament? What wouldn't they do to win it?

By the time the boys have reached the final game, even the

nonbasketball people are in the act. Cheerleaders have their nerves stretched like rubber bands. So do coachs' wives.

The greatest moment of all is victory, then the presentation of trophies.

I don't have to tell you the excitement that comes when a team comes forward to claim that trophy! They are the state champions! They have worked not only all year, but for years, to reach this moment.

Now there's a trophy shop in the city where I can buy a trophy like that. I can put it up on the shelf and show it to all my friends.

"Do you see my new trophy?" I could say.

Of course they would look at me with pity.

I'm not the state championship basketball team. I never will be.

The truth is that trophy wouldn't really be a trophy. It would merely be a cheap imitation, for I had not worked to win it. It may be identical to the one the boys received. But it's still a cheap imitation. A fake. I don't deserve it.

People would think more of the boys for having it. But they would think less of me for having it.

But there is a trophy which I can win. It's legitimate. It's for real. And it lasts forever. I would never have to dust it or polish it.

It's you. Or a friend.

"For what is our hope, or joy, or crown of rejoicing? Are not even ye in the presence of our Lord Jesus Christ at his coming? For ye are our glory and joy [trophy]" (1 Thessalonians 2:19, 20).

Our trophies in heaven are those we have won to the Saviour. They are living trophies, walking about as a shining example of the power of witnessing for Christ on earth. They are our source of greatest joy.

Let's get in the game. Let's work as hard as our sons and neighbors' sons to win our trophies, our "glory and joy."

That's worth working for, and praying for.

The Fruit of Joy

I prayed for joy,
   but He asked me to be fruitful,
   to share His Word and love
   to those who know Him not,
   and when I did,
   I found joy.

The Joy of Praying for You

Philippians 1:4 tells me that my heart fills with joy when I
  pray for you. Why is this?

Joy comes from loving you enough to pray.

Joy comes from thinking of you so that I will want to pray.

Joy comes from thinking of God so that I will want Him to
  help you.

Joy comes from bringing a needy friend and an abundant
  God together.

Joy comes from concerning myself with your needs instead
  of my own.

Joy comes from a legitimate triangle of love—God, you,
  and I.

Joy comes from lifting you up to heaven instead of dragging
  you down into the mud.

Joy comes from giving up time to pray for you.

Joy comes from the assurance that God will answer and
  help you.

Joy comes from the knowledge that joy is my only gift in
  this transaction, the only gift I truly want.

Joy comes from an opportunity to talk with my Lord about
  you.

Joy comes from asking for another, not for myself.

Joy comes from desiring more for you instead of coveting
  what you have.

Joy comes . . . so I will pray a little joy into my life by
  praying for you. Perhaps you would like to do the
  same for me.

Joy . . . Giving or Receiving

I prayed for joy,
      but He made me give
      before I could receive,
      for His gift of joy
      will follow close
      behind my gift of self.

Parting With Tears, Uniting With Joy

That's the way it happened.

When we parted, we wept.

Now you're gone and I think often about you. I remember the thoughts we shared when you were here.

There's something good about the presence of people we love. They do good things to us. They make us feel secure and warm.

But there's a time to be absent. Responsibilities call. The valley is as important as the mountain, although I'll take the mountain whenever I can. Now is the time to put into practice the many things we talked about. Now is the time to test the thoughts we knew were right.

There are some people who strike fire because they're fun, or winsome, or beautiful, or handsome, or talkative, or well-traveled, or perceptive, or something else.

You're not an expert in any of these things. You don't need to be. It's a joy to be with you because you bring me closer to God. When I'm with you, I sense His presence in you. I feel more like walking the way He wants. I feel more like praying and reading my Bible, so we can communicate more about these things.

Do you see now why we wept when we parted?

Do you see why I miss you so much now?

Of course I can pray without you.

It isn't essential that you're here so that I can think about God and read His Word.

It's just that I can do these things so much better when you are here.

That's why we wept.
That's also why I will sense a new joy when you return.
Please hurry.

Greatly desiring to see thee, being mindful of thy tears,
that I may be filled with joy. . . .

                                                    2 Timothy 1:4

The Paradox of Joy

Many of the principles that guide our Christian conduct seem paradoxical. Jesus' guidelines often seem the opposite of natural laws. For example:

The way to life is through death, and the way to death is through life.

> For whosoever will save his life shall lose it: but whosoever will lose his life for my sake, the same shall save it.
>
> Luke 9:24

The way to become a leader is to become a servant.

> . . . but whosoever will be great among you, let him be your minister; And whosoever will be chief among you, let him be your servant.
>
> Matthew 20:26, 27

The way to get is to give.

> Give, and it shall be given unto you; good measure, pressed down, and shaken together, and running over, shall men give into your bosom. For with the same measure that ye mete withal it shall be measured to you again.
>
> Luke 6:38

The way to be truly rich is to make yourself truly poor.

> Jesus said unto him, If thou wilt be perfect, go and sell that thou hast, and give to the poor, and thou shalt have treasure in heaven: and come and follow me.
>
> Matthew 19:21

The way to public rewards is through secret prayer.

> But thou, when thou prayest, enter into thy closet, and when thou hast shut thy door, pray to thy Father which is in secret; and thy Father which seeth in secret shall reward thee openly.
>
> Matthew 6:6

The way to ask for much is to pray briefly.

> But when ye pray, use not vain repetitions, as the heathen do: for they think that they shall be heard for their much speaking. Be not ye therefore like unto them: for your Father knoweth what things ye have need of, before ye ask him.
>
> Matthew 6:7, 8

So it should not come as a surprise to learn that the way to add joy is to subtract self through sacrifice and service to the Lord and others.

> Yea, and if I be offered upon the sacrifice and service of your faith, I joy, and rejoice with you all. For the same cause also do ye joy, and rejoice with me.
>
> Philippians 2:17,18

The Joy of Emptiness

I prayed for joy,
    but He required
    that I empty out myself
    so He could fill
    the vacant place
    with that for which I prayed.

The Joy of Trouble

My brethren, count it all joy when ye fall into divers temptations.

James 1:2

That's a strange thing to say, Lord.

I've always been taught to stay away from temptations and trouble. Keep away from things like that. Don't breathe their foul air, lest I be contaminated.

Now You're telling me to welcome these pests like friends. Why, Lord? Surely they are not Your friends. What good will they do me?

I know that I don't have to go looking for troubles. Or temptations. They just keep pounding on the door of my life. It's enough to keep the door closed. No, I certainly wouldn't go out looking for them. You know that, Lord.

But they do come. They visit me hourly and demand attention. "Open up," they say. "Let us in."

You don't really want me to let them in, do You, Lord? I know that's not what You're saying.

But a few of them crawl in under the door. Or through the window. I don't know how they get inside my life, Lord, but You know. They're just there. What do I do now? Should I shake hands with them? Coddle them? Bed them down and feed them? Are You asking me to do that? I don't think so.

You've told me so many times to kick them out the door. Drive them out! Fight them! Get rid of them!

That's the time for joy, isn't it, Lord? Wrestling with these things gives me strength. Thank You, Lord, for that. Kicking them out helps to make a man of me. I appreciate that, too.

Now that I'm sure You're with me and helping me, I will be

joyful. This experience has reminded me of that again. I needed that reminder. Thank You for that, Lord.

By the time I sweep out this whole unwelcome mess, I've developed some real patience. I'm grateful for that, too.

Was that what You were saying? "The testing of your faith brings out steadfastness." In full bloom, that becomes Christian character.

That's something I can't buy. But You helped me get it free.

Thanks, Lord, for helping me through this trouble and temptation. I needed this time to help me grow.

The Gift of Love . . . and Joy

I prayed for joy,
    but He sent love instead,
    His love, and that of others,
    that I might take it,
    and with it get
    the gift of joy, too.

I Could Have Been a Frog

That's right! I could have been a frog. Tonight I could be sitting on a wet lily pad, grunking at the full moon.

Of course, if I really *were* a frog, that idea would not seem so bad at all. I'm sure most frogs think other frogs are much more handsome and intelligent than those strange two-legged creatures that throw plastic frogs with strings into their back yard.

But, I'm *not* a frog.

I never was.

I never will be. I'm sure the frogs are glad. They have enough troubles with genuine frogs.

But I do get strange feelings thinking about what, or whom, I could have been. A frog. An owl. A mouse, hiding in the back closet. A stray cat, dumped out along the road on a cold winter night.

Of course, we all dream about the important people we could have been. Emperors. Kings. Presidents. Movie stars. Singers, Rich men. Famous men.

I often wonder, "Why couldn't God have passed out a little more my way in the good-looks department?" Or, "Why didn't God send a little more money my way?"

Then I have to admit. If He had, I might have become a different kind of guy. Who wants a proud, rotten heart?

There's as much honor in being a frog as a fellow with a rotten heart.

I could have been a frog, or an emperor, or a movie star. But I'm not. For some strange, wonderful reason, God sent me through the medium of parenthood and into the care of two specific people, at one specific time and place.

God didn't create me as a prince.

Or a frog!

He made me to be me.

I'll never become a king.

I'll never become a frog.

But I can become the most effective me that my talents and ambitions permit. I can work in partnership with the Creator in doing His chores on earth. I can make plans to share His home forever and ever. And I can share the route to that home with those who wander.

Let frogs be frogs.

And kings be kings.

My prayer of thanksgiving tonight is, "Lord, thank You for making me to be me. And for giving me the unlimited opportunities to share in Your Word, Yourself, Your home."

That is joy. The joy of being me and of doing what I believe He wants me to do for Him.

Joy Isn't. . . .

Joy isn't getting my way all the time.
Joy isn't getting more than others get.
Joy isn't getting every time I ask.
Joy isn't getting while others are giving.
Joy isn't getting the better end of a bargain.
Joy isn't getting more than I give.
Joy isn't getting abundant things.
Joy isn't getting more than I ask.
Joy isn't *getting*.

Joy *is* giving myself away to God and
    His friends the way He would have me do.

Raindrops on a Hot Sidewalk

Joy is . . .

Raindrops on a hot sidewalk.
A word of love at a funeral.
A child's song in a nursing home.
A rainbow after a destructive storm.
A reassuring smile from a friend you've hurt.
The first tulip, poking through the frozen soil.
A happy lesson, learned from defeat.
The song of a meadowlark on yesterday's battlefield.
A shaft of sunlight through a gray winter sky.
A Bible in a strange hotel room.
A "chance" meeting with a Christian miles from home.
A lapel pin that identifies your new boss as a Christian.

The Joy of Numberlessness

Lord, I'm so glad you didn't assign a *number* to me! You made me a little different from all others. You stamped on my fingers a print that is unlike any other among all the billions of people who have lived. You gave me a unique appearance, a mind of my own, and a will to choose You. Thank You, Lord.

I stand here rejoicing with great joy that I *am* an individual in Your eyes. You identify me easily, without a number. You even know the hairs on my head (Your job *is* getting easier every year, though). And You know my heart.

This is joy, to know a God who knows me that well . . . without one number involved.

Joy

Someone told me about this years ago. It's an old idea, but worth repeating:

J—Jesus first

O—Others next

Y—Yourself last

The Joy of Jesus

A book about joy would not be complete without considering the joy of Jesus.

I remember as a boy the sad, gloomy pictures of Him. Some showed His face twisted with pain as He suffered on the Cross.

If anyone had asked me then, "What do you think of Jesus?" I would have said, "He hurts," or "He's sad."

But the Bible says, "Looking unto Jesus the author and finisher of our faith; who for the joy that was set before him endured the cross" (Hebrews 12:2).

I know the Cross was a joy to Jesus because it was the place where He completed the work of redemption which He set out to do. The entire history of humanity focused there. The entire plan of redemption focused there. The physical suffering of Jesus must have been overshadowed by the great joy that He felt inside, knowing that He was fulfilling what He had set out to do from the very beginning.

So the pictures of a sad Jesus still don't fit into my image of Him. I like to think of Him as the Man of Joy. The Man of Sorrows drank deep of our suffering. But He knew it as His joy.

". . . we also joy in God through our Lord Jesus Christ, by whom we have now received the atonement" (Romans 5:11).

If the Cross was a place of joy to Jesus, the work He did there should certainly be an act of joy to us.

No, I can't come to the Cross with a face of mourning. I must come with my heart singing.

"We joy in God through our Lord Jesus Christ."
Why?
"By whom we have now received the atonement."
That's good news. That's The Good News.
I'm glad. In fact, I'm overflowing with joy because of it.
Aren't you?